My Hair Rocks

LaPorscha Thompson

I can wear bows, I can wear balls, I can wear ribbons, I can wear it all!

I can wear it curly...

I can wear it straight and I can wear it long to make it shake...

I can wear it up, I can wear it down...

I can wear it to the side
or swirl it all around...

I can wear a twist
or maybe a bun...
anything quick to
get the job done...

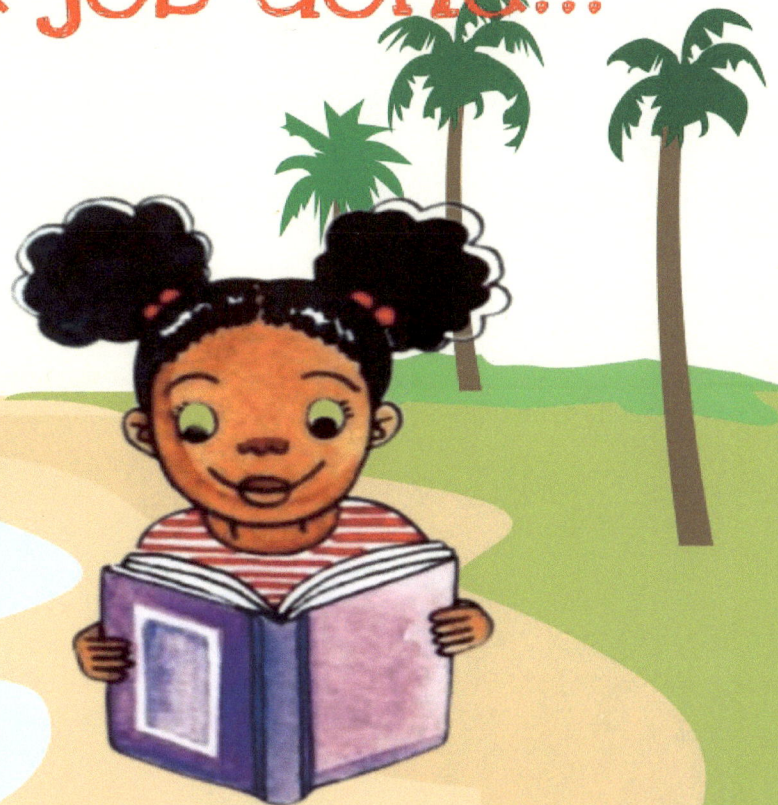

I can wear a Fro.. just let it go...

I can wear it short or even tall, either way I can wear it all...

I can wear knots,
because I like it a
lot...

I can wear blonde,
because they have
more fun...

I can even wear a
wrap to cover my
naps...

I can wear puffs, if my mom don't comb it so ruff...

I can wear red or blue...

I can wear both if
I wanted to...

I can wear it combed...
I can wear it teased...

I can wear it any
way I please...

I can wear braids...

I can wear locs...

I can wear anything because my hair rocks!

First Printing: 2019
ISBN 978-0-578-22078-9
I'Jale Publishing Co LLC
 2431 Manhattan Blvd Suite C Harvey, La. 70058
www.ijalepublishing.com

To my two beautiful daughters and all the little black girls out there. There is so much you can do to your hair.

www.ingramcontent.com/pod-product-compliance
Lightning Source LLC
LaVergne TN
LVHW072109070426
835509LV00002B/89

9780578220789